Red Hot Song Library

Christmas Songs

Sarah Watts

kevin mayhew

**kevin
mayhew**

First published in Great Britain in 2012 by Kevin Mayhew Ltd.
Buxhall, Stowmarket, Suffolk IP14 3BW
Tel: +44 (0) 1449 737978 Fax: +44 (0) 1449 737834
E-mail: info@kevinmayhewltd.com

www.kevinmayhew.com

ISBN 978 1 84867 513 1
ISMN M 57042 170 1
Catalogue No. 3612475

Cover design: Rob Mortonson
© Images used under licence from Shutterstock Inc.
Music editor: Donald Thomson

Printed and bound in Great Britain

Contents

At the Christmas bazaar

Sarah Watts

CD tracks 1 & 2

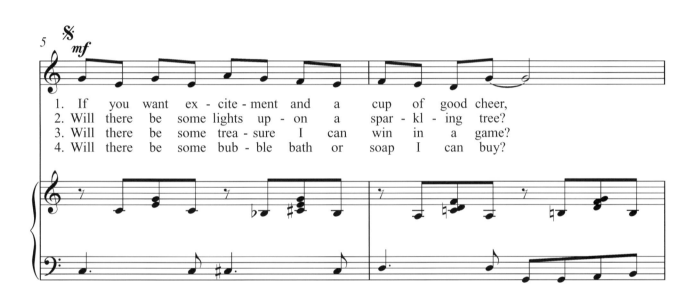

1. If you want ex - cite - ment and a cup of good cheer,
2. Will there be some lights up - on a spar - kl - ing tree?
3. Will there be some trea - sure I can win in a game?
4. Will there be some bub - ble bath or soap I can buy?

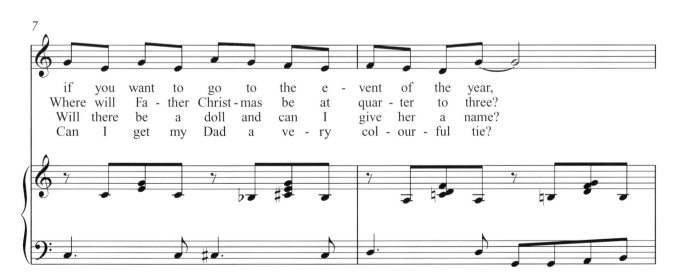

if you want to go to the e - vent of the year,
Where will Fa - ther Christ - mas be at quar - ter to three?
Will there be a doll and can I give her a name?
Can I get my Dad a ve - ry col - our - ful tie?

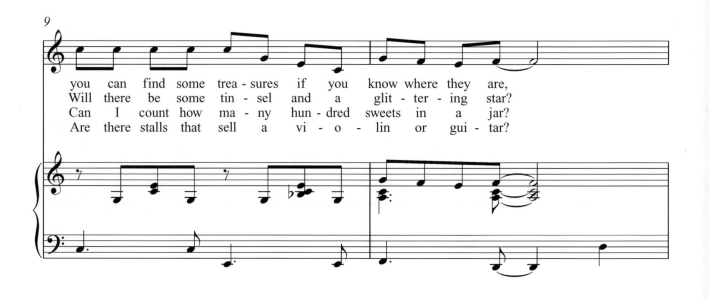

you can find some trea - sures if you know where they are,
Will there be some tin - sel and a glit - ter - ing star?
Can I count how ma - ny hun - dred sweets in a jar?
Are there stalls that sell a vi - o - lin or gui - tar?

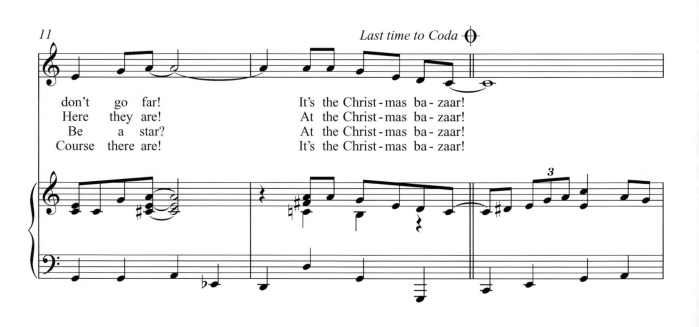

Last time to Coda

don't go far! It's the Christ - mas ba - zaar!
Here they are! At the Christ - mas ba - zaar!
Be a star? At the Christ - mas ba - zaar!
Course there are! It's the Christ - mas ba - zaar!

Refrain

Sweets and cho-co-late, a cake and mince pies;

take a luc-ky dip and get a Christ-mas sur-prise. Sing a ca-rol or a

jin - gle - bell song, a - ny - thing you need to help your

D.S. 𝄋 *CODA*

Christ-mas a-long. Christ-mas ba-zaar!

Joy to the world round

Words: Isaac Watts (1674-1748) alt.
Music: Lowell Mason (1792-1872) arr. Sarah Watts

CD tracks 3 & 4

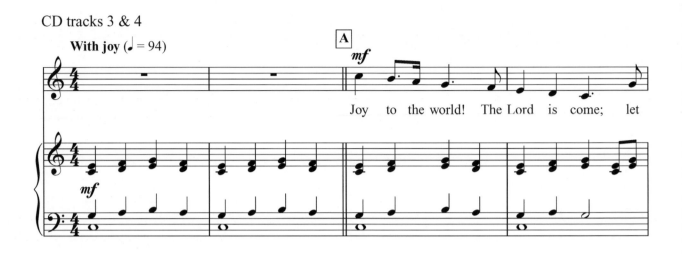

Joy to the world! The Lord is come; let

earth re-ceive her King; let ev-'ry heart pre-pare him room and

heav'n and na-ture sing, and heav'n and na-ture sing, and heav'n, and heav'n and

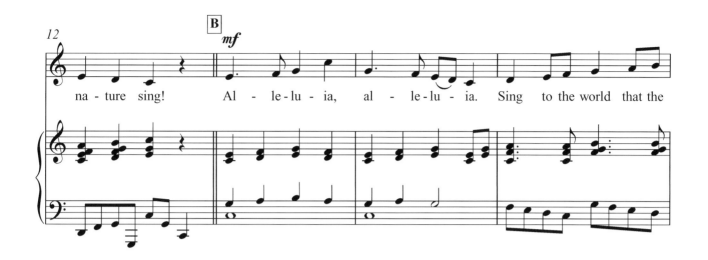

na - ture sing! Al - le -lu - ia, al - le - lu - ia. Sing to the world that the

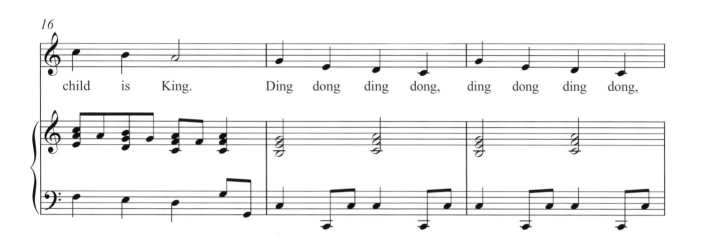

child is King. Ding dong ding dong, ding dong ding dong,

al - le - lu - ia, al - le - lu - ia; bells ring out and the an - gels sing!

This is sung as a two-part round, with the second part
entering when the first part reaches the letter 'B'.

The piano should repeat from letter 'B' to the end
to allow both parts to finish.

Happy Christmas!

Traditional
arr. Sarah Watts

CD tracks 5 & 6

Hap - py Christ - mas. Hap - py New Year too.

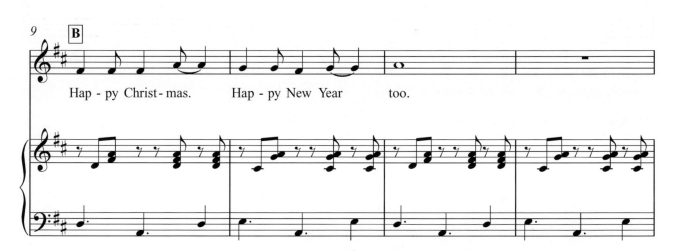

Hap - py Christ - mas. Hap - py New Year too.

Hap - py Christ - mas. Hap - py Christ - mas. Hap - py Christ - mas.

Hap - py Christ - mas. Hap - py Christ - mas. Lots of joy to

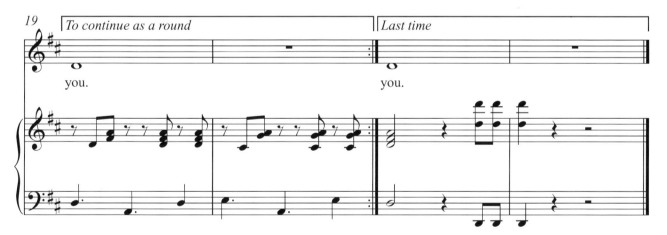

To continue as a round

Last time

you. you.

This is sung as a two-part round, with the second part
entering when the first part reaches the letter 'B'.

This peaceful time of year

Sarah Watts

CD tracks 7 & 8

I can make the date. A hun - dred days to Christ - mas, now I'd
then a Christ - mas pud. And then buy all the Christ - mas cards and
get them in the post. And then pre - pare the brus - sels sprouts, the
time is near - ly here to wish you Mer - ry Christ - mas at this

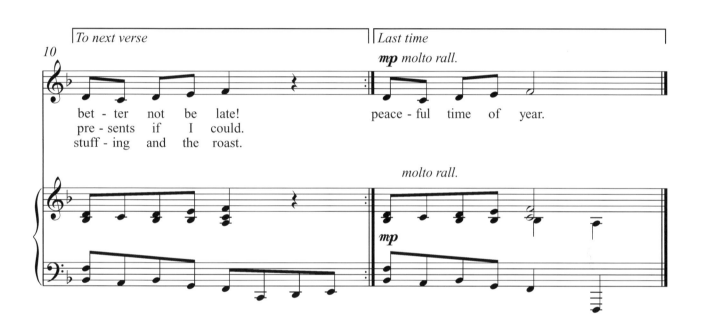

To next verse

Last time

mp molto rall.

molto rall.

mp

bet - ter not be late! peace - ful time of year.
pre - sents if I could.
stuff - ing and the roast.

Over the river and through the woods

Traditional
arr. Sarah Watts

CD tracks 9 & 10

Briskly: one-in-a-bar feel (♩. = 80)

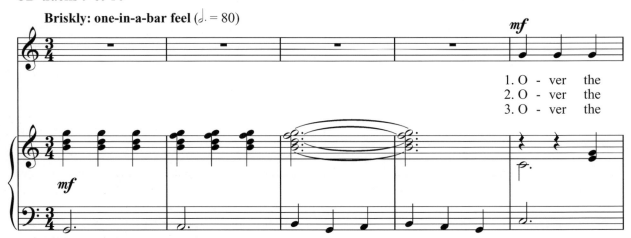

1. O - ver the
2. O - ver the
3. O - ver the

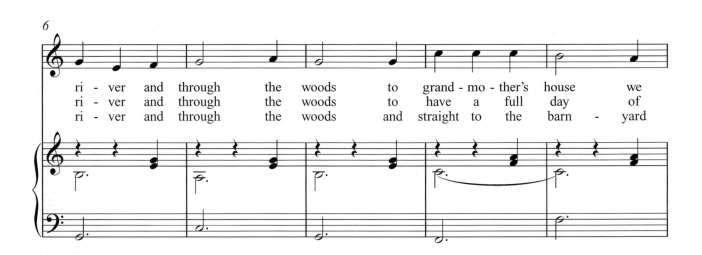

ri - ver and through the woods to grand - mo - ther's house we
ri - ver and through the woods to have a full day of
ri - ver and through the woods and straight to the barn - yard

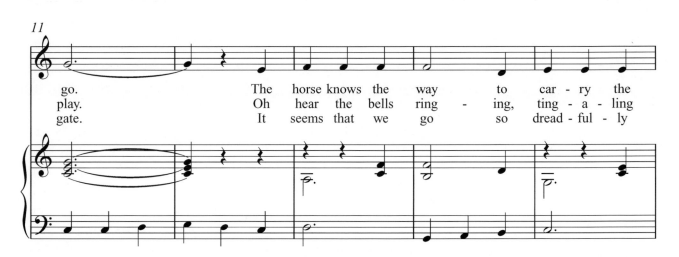

go. The horse knows the way to car - ry the
play. Oh hear the bells ring - ing, ting - a - ling
gate. It seems that we go so dread - ful - ly

sleigh through white and drift - ed snow.
ling, for it is Christ - mas Day.
slow, it is so hard to wait.

O - ver the ri - ver and through the woods, oh how the wind does
O - ver the ri - ver and through the woods, trot fast, my dap - ple
O - ver the ri - ver and through the woods, now Grand - ma's cap I

blow; it stings the toes and bites the
grey; spring o'er the ground and just like a
spy; hur - rah for fun! The pud - ding's

nose as o - ver the ground we go.
hound, for this is Christ - mas Day.
done! Hur - rah for pump - kin pie!

Wouldn't it be lovely if Christmas were tomorrow?

Sarah Watts

CD tracks 11 & 12

With sentiment and rhythmic flexibility (♩ = 72)

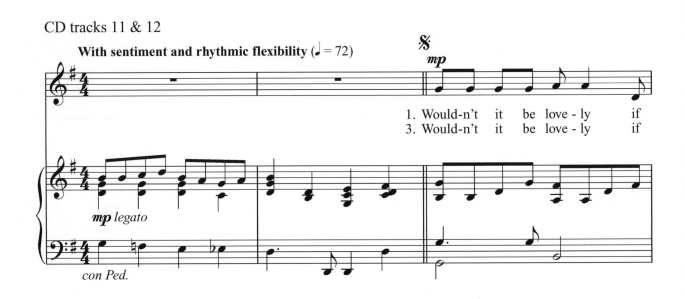

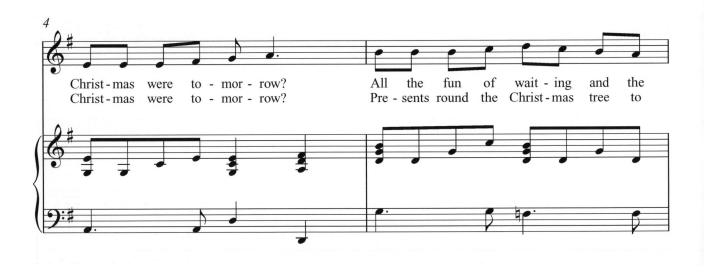

ca - rol sing - ers sing - ing, oh would - n't it be won - der - ful if
all the world was peace - ful, oh would - n't it be nice if it was

To continue

now was Christ - mas Eve?

Last time
rall.
Fine

al - ways Christ - mas Eve?
rall.

2. Would - n't it be love - ly if

Christ - mas were to - mor - row? Christ - mas lights in win - dows and the

hol - ly be - ing hung.   Would-n't it be love-ly   if

it was near - ly mid-night,   the snow was fall-ing qui-et-ly and

D.S. al Fine

bells were be - ing rung.

Infant holy, infant lowly

Words: Traditional Polish, trans. Margaret Gellibrand Reed (1885-1933)
Music: Sarah Watts

CD tracks 13 & 14

wing - ing an-gels sing - ing, no-wells ring - ing, tid-ings bring - ing; Christ the

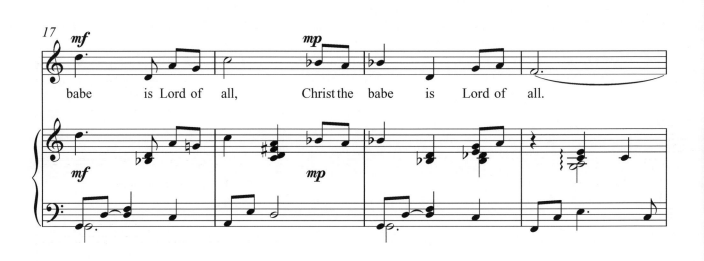

babe is Lord of all, Christ the babe is Lord of all.

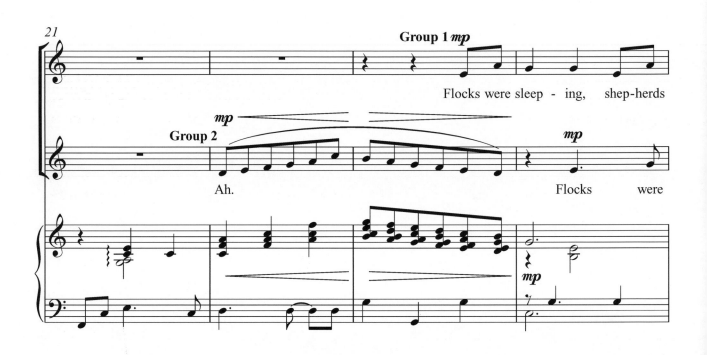

Group 1 *mp*

Flocks were sleep - ing, shep-herds

Group 2 *mp*

Ah. Flocks were

you, Christ the babe was born for you.

you, Christ the babe was born for you.

In-fant ho - ly, in-fant low - ly, for his

In-fant ho - ly, in-fant low - ly, for his

bed a cat-tle stall; ox-en low - ing, lit-tle know - ing Christ the

bed a cat-tle stall; ox-en low - ing, lit-tle know - ing Christ the

23

Let's have a very good Christmas

Sarah Watts

CD tracks 15 & 16

- deer.　　　Let's　see the　stars from a sleigh.　　　　Oh,　let's　have a　ve-ry good

Christ - mas.　　　Let's have a　won-der-ful day.

To continue

Last time

This is sung as a two-part round, with the second part
entering when the first part reaches the letter 'B'.

Ding dong! merrily on high round

Words: George Ratclifffe Woodward (1848-1934)
Music: Traditional French melody arr. Sarah Watts

CD tracks 17 & 18

1. Ding dong! mer-ri-ly on high, in heav'n the bells are ring - ing; ding dong! ve-ri-ly the
2. E'en so here be-low, be-low, let stee-ple bells be swung - en, and i - o, i-o, i-
3. Pray you, du-ti-ful-ly prime your ma-tin chime, ye ring - ers; may you beau-ti-ful-ly

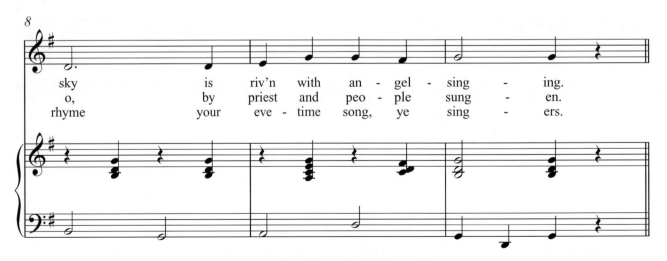

sky is riv'n with an - gel - sing - ing.
o, by priest and peo - ple sung - en.
rhyme your eve - time song, ye sing - ers.

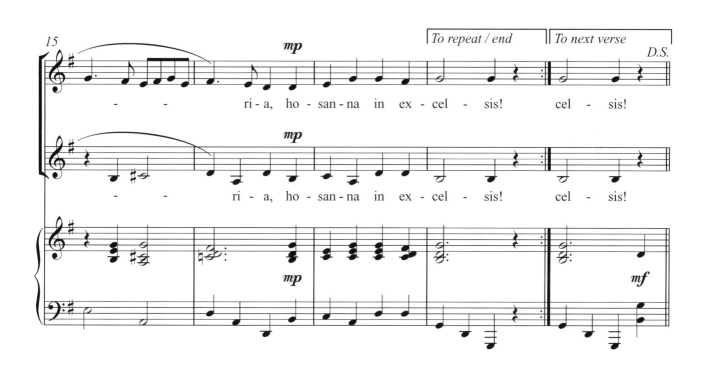

A fowl Christmas

Words: Rowena Gibbons
Music: Sarah Watts

CD tracks 19 & 20

1. 'What are you do-ing for Christ-mas?' said the tur-key to the
2. 'How ve-ry sca-ry! Oh hea-vens!' gasped the goose, 'Oh dea-rie
3. 'I think that we'd bet-ter scar-per' they a-greed, and so that

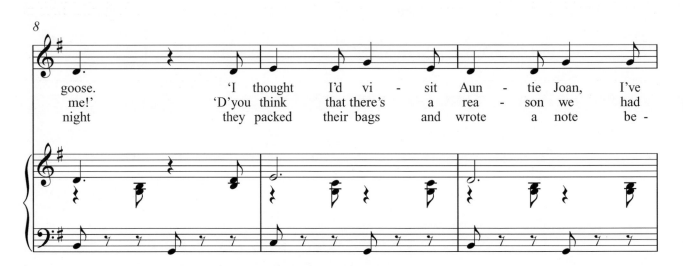

goose. 'I thought I'd vi-sit Aun-tie Joan, I've
me!' 'D'you think that there's a rea-son we had
night they packed their bags and wrote a note be-

11

heard she's on the loose.
ca - vi - ar for tea?
fore they both took flight:

mp *cresc.*

Al - though the food was
And pink cham-pagne and
'We're sor - ry that we've

14

ve - ry good where she's been kept since May,
straw - b'rry tart for af - ters, what a treat!
left you af - ter all, you've done a lot

mf

she
But
but

17

says she's got a hunch she might not be there Christ - mas
now, on se - cond thoughts, may - be it was - n't quite so
act - ual - ly we've no de - sire to go in - to the

20

Day.'
sweet!'
pot!'

f

The hurry-up Christmas song

Sarah Watts

CD tracks 21 & 22

Sing a

mer-ry old Christ - mas song; it will help all the days a - long.

With a bun-dle of fun and a cup of good cheer, it's the

The holly and the Christmas pud

Michael Trefold and Billy Mitton
arr. Sarah Watts

CD tracks 23 & 24

Jolly! (♩ = 138)

What three things at Christ-mas time can make you feel so good?

Ho ho ho, the mis-tle-toe, the hol-ly and the Christ-mas pud!

What three things make peo-ple feel the way that peo-ple should?

Ho ho ho, the mis - tle - toe, the hol - ly and the Christ - mas pud! Now we've

heard some nice sug - ges - tions, but I'm sure you'll all a - gree that we

don't want twen - ty ques - tions so I'm on - ly ask - ing three, see!

What three things at Christ - mas mean what on - ly Christ - mas should?

Ho ho ho, the mis - tle - toe, the hol - ly and the Christ - mas pud!

Jingle bells round

James Pierpoint (1822-1893)
arr. Sarah Watts

*This is sung as a two-part round, with the second part
entering when the first part reaches the letter 'B'.*

*Sing as many times as you like; the piano continues
playing from 'A' to 'B' until everybody has finished.*

CD tracks 25 & 26

With gusto! (♩ = 165)

Rid - ing through the for - est on a one - horse o - pen sleigh;

shout - ing to the folks we know and laugh - ing all the way.

Friends come out to greet us as we're glid - ing through the snow;

Until we meet next year

Words: Sarah Watts
Music: Traditional Scottish melody
arr. Sarah Watts

CD tracks 27 & 28

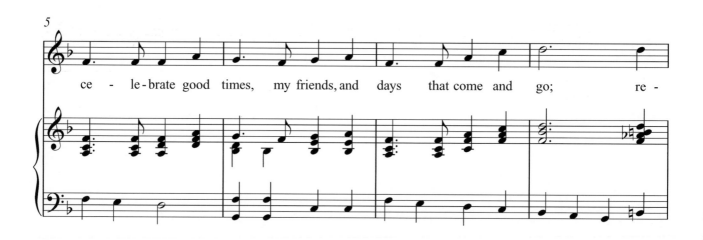

thank - ful now for all good things, good friends a - round us here; look

for - ward to the days to come when we meet a - gain next year. Be year.

This is a modern version of 'Auld lang syne' which is traditionally sung to bring in the New Year.

How about singing it at the end of term, or the end of a concert? It is traditional to link arms as it is sung.

A big fat Christmas round

Sarah Watts

*This is sung as a four-part round with parts starting
four bars apart. The accompaniment will continue
until all parts have finished.*

*How about starting the round fast, and get slower
as more and more food is consumed?*

CD tracks 29 & 30

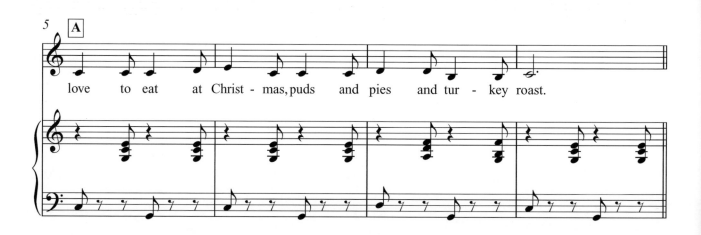

love to eat at Christ - mas, puds and pies and tur - key roast.

Par - snips and po - ta - toes, they're the things I like the most. A

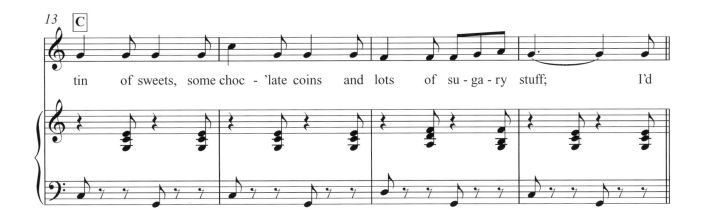

tin of sweets, some choc - 'late coins and lots of su - ga - ry stuff; I'd

keep on eat - ing choc - 'late till I think I'd had e - nough.

Christmas cacophony

Words: Traditional
Music: Sarah Watts

CD tracks 31 & 32

Ostinatos

Instrumental bass line

Last time

A tune can be improvised over the accompaniment using these notes:

The repeated Ostinatos can accompany the whole song and may be introduced or removed one at a time as an introduction or ending.

They can be sung or played on instruments.

This song can be as flexible as you like, and instruments can be used alongside or without the vocal line.

Be creative with the elements to make your own interpretation.

Christmas bells round

Sarah Watts

CD tracks 33 & 34

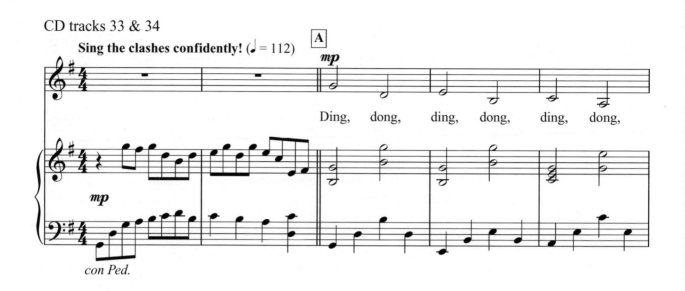

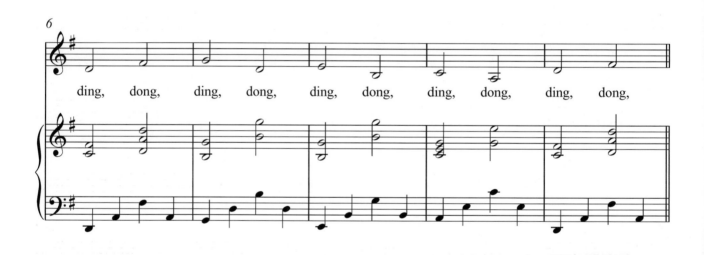

This is sung as a three-part round; the piano should keep repeating
from bar 19 to bar 26 until everybody has finished.

Christmas Day is coming

Words: Mike Cashman
Music: Sarah Watts

CD tracks 35 & 36

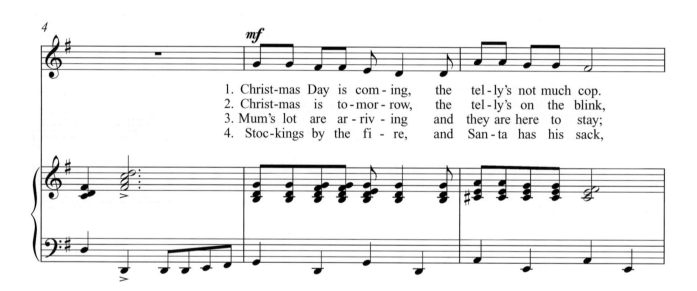

1. Christ-mas Day is com - ing, the tel - ly's not much cop.
2. Christ-mas is to-mor - row, the tel - ly's on the blink,
3. Mum's lot are ar - riv - ing and they are here to stay;
4. Stoc-kings by the fi - re, and San - ta has his sack,

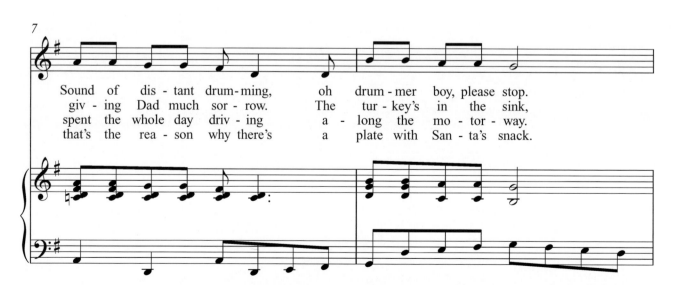

Sound of dis - tant drum-ming, oh drum - mer boy, please stop.
giv - ing Dad much sor - row. The tur - key's in the sink,
spent the whole day driv - ing a - long the mo - tor - way.
that's the rea - son why there's a plate with San - ta's snack.

Ca - rol sing - gers sing - ing, the tune is slight - ly wrong. The
Mum says it's de - frost - ing be - cause we bought it late. And
Un - cle's slight - ly grum - py, the cou - sins in a mood; and
Mum shares sweets out fair - ly, the cou - sins start to play. So

ra - di - o keeps play - ing a Christ - mas pud - ding song.
Dad says 'What's it cost - ing?' while chok - ing on a date.
Dad is get - ting jum - py, while Mum makes lots of food.
have we real - ly near - ly ar - rived at Christ - mas Day?

Silent night round

Words: Joseph Mohr (1792-1848) trans. John Freeman Young (1820-1885)
Music: Franz Grüber (1787-1863) arr. Sarah Watts

*This is sung as a two-part round, with the second part
entering when the first part reaches the letter 'B'.*

*The piano should repeat from letter 'B' to the end
to allow the second part to finish.*

CD tracks 37 & 38

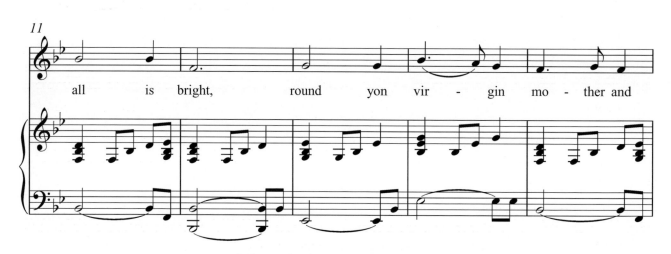

child; ho - ly in - fant, so ten - der and mild,

sleep in hea - ven-ly peace, sleep in

hea - ven-ly peace. On a hill - side near

Beth - le - hem, shep - herds watched as the an - gels

47

came.   O - ver a   sta - ble   a   star   shone bright,   to

show   that a   King   had been   born   that   night.

Christ,   the   Sa - viour is   born,

Christ,   the   Sa - viour is   born.

To continue   D.S.   Last time

6 Minute Nativity

A mini-musical

Words: Rowena Gibbons
Music: Sarah Watts

CD tracks 39 & 40

There was once a girl called Ma-ry and she lived in Ga-li-lee, where one

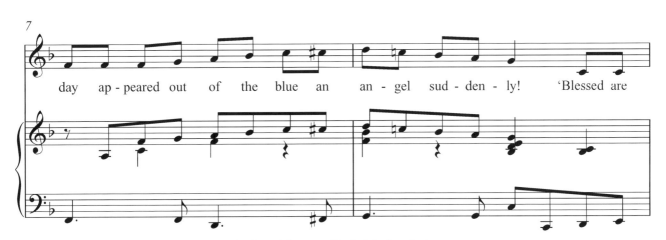

day ap-peared out of the blue an an-gel sud-den-ly! 'Blessed are

you a - mong all wo - men, you shall be God's cho - sen one, pret - ty

soon you'll have a ba - by who'll be Je - sus, God's own

Son!' 'Oh my

soul doth mag - ni - fy the Lord' cried Ma - ry, full of joy, and she went to tell her boy - friend Jo - seph

of the ba-by boy. 'Oh my good-ness, how ex-cit-ing, but it may be kind of tough, 'cos to

Beth-le-hem we're go-ing and that's dif-fi-cult e-nough.'

Off to Beth-le-hem they tra-velled with the

ba-by al-most due; they'd to go and pay their tax-es at the In-land Re-ve-nue. But there

wasn't a-ny room in a-ny inn for them to stay, so they spent it in a sta-ble with a

ba - by on the way! Al - so

look - ing at the stars that night were shep - herds with their sheep, but there

wasn't a-ny chance that they'd be get-ting a-ny sleep 'cos the an-gel came and said to them 'Get

45

up and go and see, in a sta-ble o-ver yon-der is the first na-ti-vi-ty.'

48 **Swing** (♩ = 106) (♫ = ♩ ♪)

mf

52

'It has been a fun-ny sort of night', the ass said to the ox. 'First the

55

cou-ple, then the ba - by, now some guys have left their flocks and are

kneel - ing at our man - ger where the babe's a - sleep on hay; guess he

must be some-thing spe-cial 'cos they've called this Christ - mas

Day!'

70 **Dreamily** (♩. = 58)

pp

Then three wise men heard a - bout the birth of

pp

con Ped.

74

Je - sus from a - far. 'We must go and see the ba - by: look, let's

78

fol - low that bright star!' So they set off on their ca - mels and they jour-neyed night and

83 *molto dim.*

ppp

day o - ver hill and vale and moun - tain to the sta - ble far a - way.

molto dim.

ppp

55

But the wise men thought King Her-od was an e - vil, hor-rid chap and they said to one an-o-ther, 'We must get a dif-f'rent map 'cos we think that old King Her-od is a nas-ty, jea-lous man; there-fore let's re-turn an-o-ther way and spoil his cun-ning plan!'

So they tra-velled e - ver on - ward, guid - ed by that same bright star and it took them to the sta - ble 'It's our jour - ney's end, *hur - rah!* Now let's

(Spoken)

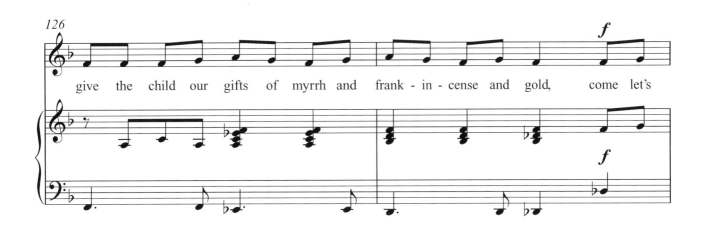

give the child our gifts of myrrh and frank - in - cense and gold, come let's

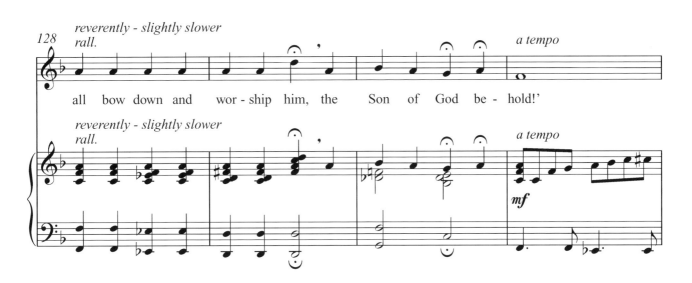

all bow down and wor - ship him, the Son of God be - hold!'

59

Red Hot Song Library

christmas Songs